Stone

Stone

John Unterecker

The University Press of Hawaii ⚶
Honolulu

Poems in this collection have appeared in *Ark River Review*, *The Anglo-Welsh Review*, *The Arts in Ireland*, *Bird Effort*, *CAIM*, *Choice*, *The Greenfield Review*, *The Hawaii Review*, *Interstate*, *Modern Poetry Studies*, *Poetry Ireland*, *Poetry Northwest*, *Poetry Now*, *Quarterly Review of Literature*, *Shenandoah*, *Southern Poetry Review*, and *Wind*.

Copyright © 1977 by The University Press of Hawaii

Manufactured in the United States of America

Library of Congress Cataloging in Publication Data

Unterecker, John Eugene, 1922-
    Stone.

    I. Title.
PS3571.N8S7   811'.5'4   77-26078
ISBN 0-8248-0492-9

Contents

Preface

Most of these poems are about Ireland or were written in Ireland. The place names give it away: Drumholm—not even a village, just a dozen scattered houses on the windswept Donegal coast near Ballintra; Sligo, the West-of-Ireland town Yeats grew up in and dreamed always of returning to; Dublin, with its National Museum and pubs and soft voices and softer rain.

Yet these poems are about Ireland only superficially. Their real landscape is the one inside my head that superimposes on Western New York State, where I lived until I went off to college, all the other places in which pressures of intense feeling made mountain or sea or sky vivid: Silver Creek, Grafton, and Schenectady in New York State; Williamsport in Pennsylvania; Collioure and Foix in France; Drumholm, Renvyle, Sligo, and Clifden in Ireland; Honolulu, where I am writing this note, and where—thinking originally of Hawaiian petroglyphs—I started the second poem in this book. The landscapes tumble over each other to form a conglomerate landscape, interior and unpredictable.

Similarly, the time of these poems is more often than not a jumble of private crisis points. If I were to make a graph of my emotional history, it would look something like a stock-market chart with peak years hitting in early childhood, in middle adolescence, and at increasingly frequent intervals ever since then. The interactions of these times of greater-than-usual feeling fuel most of these poems. There is no real *present* in them, only an overlap of vanished but not discarded *nows*.

The primary energy of these Irish poems comes, therefore, from places and times that are, on the whole, not Irish. And yet none of them could have been written if I hadn't spent one winter in Malahide and a part of another in Drumholm—or, for that matter, four summers in and around Sligo.

All of these poems, I believe, stand by themselves. But for persons unfamiliar with Irish legend and Irish geography, I've appended a set of very brief informational notes. In these notes, I have also credited prior publication and identified the living persons mentioned in a number of the poems.

Though my debts of gratitude are many, I want particularly to thank my editor, Gary L. Cooper, for unusually generous and insightful help in preparing the manuscript; the directors and trustees of Yaddo and of the John Simon Guggenheim Memorial Foundation for providing me congenial times and places in which to compose poems; and two poets, Martha Webb and Jim Kraus, whose work I love and whose long conversations while I was organizing this book helped shape not just a sequence of poems but, as well, the author who wrote them.

Stone

The Burn

A tiny scar just off the life line:—a kind of cucumber, 1/4 inch long, 1/8 inch wide.
''Call it stigmata.''   ''Not on your life—off center.''
''Call it a cigarette burn.''

.   .   .   .

At 37,000 feet, land edges in: 9:15:   wrist wrong.
        (It is dusk in Ireland, afternoon in Labrador.)   Change time.

.   .   .   .

    Shed: cover/uncover

        Ten hours: I have shed Sligo by two days, Mountrath by one:
        ''I am beginning to shed Dublin.''
        (Patrick Street: St. Patrick's.   Goodbye, Swift.)

            —to remove a covering (as skin)   /   a lean-to (flimsy as faith)

                        ''Shed of God''

            motor idling   door slam   ''Write.''

                        Nobody's home.

.   .   .   .

"Keep time," I say to my wrist,
   and it listens to Greek dances on a Donegal field,
   night voices by a Connemara lake.

   (The dancer is the song inside my wrist: I know that dancer's name:
   grace is a gesture we must learn to bear.)

   Friends, I have lost faith: 37,000 feet straight down:
   I fly on artificial wings, mine gone.

"Burn this," I think.
   It will explode.   I saw a barn burn once,
   a flare against the Pennsylvania night. I was young:

   a kind of gathering, embers
   swaying pell-mell toward black.

My reach is emptiness.
   In a week, the scar will be gone:
   an absence burning the palm of my hand.

Who doesn't press his mouth against fire, then lick the wound, flying home?

Gunsight

I see men walking into the mountains.

The first man carries a thing. His fingers are bent,
an articulation of knuckles. If he were carrying a cross,
the footprints staggering behind him would be deeper.

Black crows on a woven sky.

One man has dropped his rifle. His left hand
picks up a fistful of twigs. He brushes them
on the horizon, painting.

Elk border the margins of this song. But they are wary.

Three men walking abreast whisper
—or do I hear their blood whispering
through roped arteries?

A skin of ice, fish shadowy.

I have seen the last two figures in dream:
a boy, an old man.
One leads the other, perhaps drags him through snow.

These men walk into a narrow darkness that is between mountains.

At Renvyle

On a windy day, the generous earth
gives us this green hollow
out of the wind.

Sounds come close
green on the wind, grass, the sea mumbling among stone,
far off, a cartload of stones, tumbling.

A man who had sailed all the geographies of love might come here on any blue day
to hear clouds opening into light
or, breathing, the blue requiems of sea.

But would he rest in the sun
listening to the hungriest speech of the place:
bleached bone, stone, feathers, a smashed oar?

The tide breaks rock,
a woman beautiful and angry as the sea
singing of heartbreak.

Below the Cliffs, Donegal

Floodtide runs out.
A swimmer
walking on stone.
Absence.

Nothing we say can undo the brutal tenderness of such long light.

Tír Conaill

Here in the love-sick darkness of a windy night trees buckle in wind,
trees bend above stone. *Who is to say we have not stumbled on Grania's bed,*
a torn moon entangling branches? Two stones
stretch out like lovers in this broken light: *Diarmiud and Grania's*
flesh.   Time runs out.
We have wandered out of summer, out of evasions,
into cold air. Nothing troubles this place but blown trees.
Where else can truth be found if not in the cold stone that held such famous lovers until dawn?

Before Dawn

I try to remember the shape of the gale.
There is nothing left of the gale but a broken branch.
It leans against moonlight:
a jealous lover's harsh song.

Beach

There are three figures:

A young man writing on sand,
    an older man, camera in hand, walking the dunes
        (I have become that man. He is a stranger.),

a girl leading a black horse down the cliff path.
    Where the steep path narrows, he rears.
        He is a stallion, his black hooves cutting the air.

The sun is a spotlight:

A haze on the sea, on the coast, but in the abrupt bay sunlight.
    It stands in a white column, rigid as stone. I could carve it. Near the base,
        sands are mist.   The column sheds light as if light were a statement
                written on sand.

August:

Or is it in a warp of time that I see a black horse galloping, its mane blown back by the
                wind, the girl's hair blown back,
    a black horse bursting through columns of light, hooves slashing words,
        horse, rider, sand one glare?

Annick, I have placed you here on this coast,
having no diagram of floating weeds
or patterned swans.

The mirror-writing in the camera spells a name:
        Ann? Anna. Yet hair is blown on the wind, Annick,
                and wind is a translator prodigal as sea:

Roger's words sweep up in clouds of changing light
        and thousands of gaunt stallions charge through sky.
                My lens is blind: blown sand.

Can we be honest?
Compare these life lines, gaunt on three hands.
I pick my way among words, stumbling.

Hands meet, part.
Meet.   Part.
Stone patch.

On a day in late summer, I sat at the base of a cliff watching Roger
Conover write on Donegal sand. Annick Chapoy, a girl I barely
knew, was in Paris. There was no sunlight, no mist. A stranger
who wore a small pack worked down the cliff. He approached me.
We did not speak. We did not acknowledge that we were two of
three figures on that beach.

August 22

Here at the edge of nowhere and the sea
you wind a thread of seaweed on your wrist.

''Now I belong to this place.''

Like a coil of sandy hair
it loops the blue pulse of stretched skin.

Salt tides stretch out into the blue salt darkness of the sea.

Song at Drumholm

My liveliest self, I give you fair leave
in these windblown weathers,
heather-hearted and human and strange,
to turn every blackberry corner
of yesterday's summer.

The robin, singing her love-me-forever,
kiss-catch-clutch-in-the-heather
blues, sings tide flow
and autumn's turning and white
winds folding.

Cattle along all hedges wind winter
into their frosty
breathing, their slow eyes dreaming
barn, bullock, and fodder
under all hedges.

But sea cave and sycamore tell us the world
is wider than weather.
Blackberries darken the corners
I turn, and gold seas turning
darken, darken.

My liveliest self, my other, Godspeed
on our farings.
The bronze path at evening.   Toward summer,
then.   My hand, your hand—
as if first meeting.

Apology at Midnight

Who hasn't run his hand across the do-not-touch stone hand
or—ever so gentle—brushed, as if they could be brushed back, bronze curls?

I want to say, ''I am sorry''; but the unfolding of a hand stops breath in my throat.

What is left is the stillness: leaves less dimensional than sky
and Hokusai's breaking wave—emperors ago a curved brightness—broken leaves falling.

Natural History

1

Tyrannosaurus rex snarling from the left;
Saber-tooth tiger defiant on a high limb,
below him a sea of type. Overleaf
caveman, hairy in hairier skins
(tiger's?), draws on cave wall man's
battle with bison. They were my dream life,
and in rare dreams they still are. In dream loam,
fossil trees fruit; grave fronds uncoil, lift.

2

I wonder, now, if they were not part
of a larger American dream we all shared
growing up. *Man triumphant* was the theme not just of my brown book
but of the Museum of Science, where we watched papier-mâché dogs,
cows, horses learn to wag,
to be milked, to plow; where wood and rock
yielded to conqueror man; where the air
learned to bear his starved heart.

3

In Dublin's National Museum, the dead past
leads a different life. Man's conquests are over man
or over man's nature, his artifacts those of war
or of faith, his achievements—sometimes—grace.
Burial bracelets hoop swords.
                                        To pass
from man to animal in Dublin, one walks
around the block, entering by a back door. The plan
is plain: extinction stares one in the face.

16

4

Reindeer, banded lemming, hyena, bear,
wolf, mastodon, arctic fox, great Irish deer:
Ireland's doomed mammals, in random order,
greet one at the door, *Homo sapiens* in a guard's
uniform, leaning above the bones, bored.
Wolves—one of the last to go—were
still running in packs when Swift wore
himself out. Yet no man saw more than bones of the great Irish deer.

5

Perhaps that's it—that man arrived
so late—that accounts for a sense of ease,
an acceptance of the land . . . or that Ireland spawned
no carnivore large enough to attack the great Irish deer
in his fog world, boggy and green,
where he lifted huge antlers, eleven feet broad.
Were mine an Irish dream, I would see rise
over the horizon those herds, immense against sky.

6

Or I would dream their deaths in Ballybetagh Bog,
their delicate hooves mired in the yielding moss,
great antlers like antennae searching. In the dream
silence, I would see the hundred strayed beasts
pantomime death, until at the last
only tossing antlers marred a scene
desolate and pure. So eloquent a loss.
Night after demanding night they would brush past me, grey forms thrust from grey fog.

Irish Winter

There is a darkness vaster than darkness of soul
broods over green Ireland: hollowing out graves,
it settles into pregnant flesh, unfolds
itself, furry as soot, in carved doorways.
Darker—and more Celtic—than twilight lies,
it thrust Yeats, at the end, into the cold
laughter he called truth, then pressed like a grave
truth itself, Yeats dead, to level Coole.

When Ireland was improved, henge stones were smashed
to make rubble for roads. Today the roads
smash through raths, drain holy wells.
Yet the smashed truth of place lives on
in ruined stones, flows through lives
grown dark on rivers of stout: ''Well,
I'll be dead in four or five years, thank God.''
Who hasn't heard Ireland singing its epitaph?

Though the house is gone, some of the walls
of the walled garden of Coole still stand—
a garden Yeats' daughter hated. On summer nights
guests, before signing the autograph tree,
would be brought through a red door to hear
the garden's crystal echo. ''Yeats,''
I said, one winter evening. The wind
rustled holly. ''Yeats,'' answered the ruined walls.

18

Yet there is no echo in that ritual hole
under Newgrange where on cold solstice dawns
sun's earliest ray sparks from whatever dark
pool lies in the great stone trough
a flash of reflected light, a breath
on carved walls.   I spoke.

The hungry walls swallowed my word whole.

A darkness in the hollow of a fist, in the hollows
of sheila-na-gig high on abbey walls,
the consuming darkness of Newgrange rises
like black mist over bogwater dark as stout.
More elemental than a darkness in the soul, a great
stone darkness sways over Ireland's glazed
green land. Laughter must be cold that builds
with stone towers of the stubborn soul.

North of Collioure, North of Dublin, North of Malahide

Alien, I unlock a door, calling it *home*
or manage to construct from inhabitant dogs
familiar wags and wiles. In fact, I am alone.
Perhaps it has always been the same kind of alone—
yet, in unfamiliar air, it explores me in new ways,
poisons the vestibules of my ears with a speech
gentle and clean. I rinse my lies
toward definition in this foreign hush.

Surely a rubbing landscape tongues
sharp passion. The gulls balance
on a flight of turf-scented air, print
W's on the sun. (*M's* print
the ground.) *I am on my way to France.*
These Irish gulls spell a rare word—
untranslatable, I think; I rinse
untranslatable vowels through the beak of a bird.

Precise passion may speak perfect rhyme
(*W's* against the sun). Yet *I am on
my way to France* in its long becoming
arranges a precision of its own: *Come,*
the ship is always crying, *down
and up,* a rocking rhythm, the waves
sliding under, measure, time's tune.
A tick-tock form informs our lives.

A gull shifts on the wind and its *M*,
immense as death, comes scything across waves,
across strand, darkening cliff and tower. Pure form,
a thing of light, it herds the formless
sheep into a crying corner. They shove
between tumbling sea and tumbled wall,
an earthwork built, antiquarians believe,
by a primitive, lost race. Then the gull calls—

a harsh, aggressive cry.
                    Oh, I am here,
all right—going to France—here, where you,
going nowhere, defend a broken fort, an empty tower,
a spit of pasture thrust in the sea. You tower
into the sky, circling up. I acknowledge you.
I acknowledge the defining cry. You are alone,
too—though we participate in a dance: you move;
I stand, going to France. We share the sun.

Morning

The bay is a jumble of wind.
Wind smashes in among the breakers,
a fist smashing them backwards. What jumbled light!

Or that time when we were children,
you bent over the mirror.

A Poem for Liam Miller

1

Though threads of the green year fray, a brittle mist
knits dream to frozen sleep.
                              At Phil Ryan's corner, midnight needles click
in silvering gutters.
                      I walk from Christmas to Dublin,
pass moondrifts of reluctant snow.
                                   A crisp glaze
balances night's frost-breath song: *The Croppy Boy* sighs
in tin-whistle dream down Seventh Avenue and Lower Baggot Street.
                                                      Phil Ryan's pub––

dark but for shatterings in the blind grate—
unravels smoky anecdotes, as if there were a speech for darkness and for dust.

2

Handkerchieves—
              bandages on mouths—
                                  blackening. . .
    O'Connell Bridge: ''Match?''
    Westland Row: ''Cigarette?''
    Post Office: ''Match there?''
    Amiens Street: ''Care for a . . . cigarette?''

Light blossoming like rosebuds
                           (shrouded eyes, questions) . . .
                                                  darkening.

    .   .   .   .

Where Seventh Avenue meets Broadway, memory fogs to a montage:
"She had vanished into the fog," he reported. . . .

                                          Traffic at Standstill. . . .

On Foggy Malahide Strand: Mistakes Bull for Bench (Will Recover, Say Surgeons). . . .
I paste green phrases on a phone-book subway map.
("We will not sleep this night," she had said. "You will see us lining the rails of the ship;
you will see us at dawn searching the grey fog for the first green hill of the green coast of
    Kerry," a girl with a voice like the sea, a girl with a voice like the sea rising in seasurge,
    falling, rising in seasurge.)
In Galway City, the boy who had stood us an ale—
and who sang, in a voice pure as rain, *The Croppy Boy*—fell, singing.

                             —So many voices shape the green collage.

3

Liam, your sentences suffer a sea-change, crossing the sea.
I hear them shape to my mouth.
You speak of a clock without hands: Paris/Dublin,
elastic hours of necessary speech.

                        But I am hungry for the gauze speech of Dublin
that, soft as porter, darkens in the mouth.
A steep wind blurs the unravelling voice of the sea.

Dublin Evening, Afternoon near Clifden

I am trying to act my age, an illusionist in a grey cloak.
September berries darken the hedges. Salmon thrash upstream.

At night, the city discovers its form,
a brightness on the horizon; close up,
eyes are wild in headlights, stretched skin laughing.

Headlights are hard as bone. There's a taste of skin on things.
Are they beautiful? Their faces
are carved on night. Their mouths are laughing.

I focus on the hedge. Here we are voices,
the stream full of voices and spawning salmon.

An illusionist deals in things: death in small packages,
the price of a pint of Harp. Smoke closes down
space.   A crowd of eight men

grey as smoke shape to a woman's mouth.
She knows their names. She speaks:
they are a projection on dense air,

a new-born hero floating in the pub. I watch him,
his chameleon body ignorant as dream.
Inside my cloak, I am sure of my own skin,

denier.   Yet infant gestures
charm.   She
dandles him blithely, her mouth red above a red sweater.

We fit extension rings under the lens: the hedgerow is a dark landscape:
obsidian fields.   Grey standing stones dominate the place.

Beyond the horizon, a stream
leaps rock to rock, fish leap steep water.

        Time:
        ''You don't have to be old when your face is easy,''
        Jane says, who is four and at ease in her loves.

Night's cloak lies like a dark dream on the city.

The photograph is rinsed in light,
as if the gods had spoken easy words
in a clean light's embrace.

Bridge: Sligo

1

Now the river empties
    water weeds and swans,
        oars, clouds,

a flow that tugs at the shore
    emptying, emptying
        the trailed scarf of stained water.

2

I lean over the bridge.
I burn on a disc of smoking oil.
There is nowhere for the river to go.
The ocean has filled up.
Weeds are my green hair, wavering.
At the edge of hair, brown gulls, circling, waver.

3

The tide's blunt tongue has begun to push into the mouth of the river.
The swollen salt tide slides over the river tongue
      exploring   dallying
then, trembling, pushes into the long throat.

4

Off toward America, an autumn sun sinks into cold Atlantic waves.
Already Moscow is asleep.   Wind-swept Asian plains stretch out beneath a snow-
                                          dimmed moon.

We are all bruised by the tides.

The city's lights are laughter on dark water.
On either side of the river song sweetens evening.

Rivers, High Places

1 . The Garravogue, Sligo

. . . a palisade of reeds . . .

Our voices are eased out along slow mirrors . . .

Stars.   *Fish.*   *Frogs.*

Our voices stroke the black reeds,
    push in among the tall black grasses.

The silence eases underneath our words.
    The river is a listening dream.

2 . Above Lough Allen

. . . or on a high place, pressing into light,
as if the light of the place were its own voice speaking . . .

We have climbed past tumbled cottages, past bracken,
    out upon stone and heather and light.
Here, drowned in light, we can risk dark waters.

Focus on grey rock.
  I twist fingers on the lens as if they were my own.

A source . . .   *a beginning.*

  The rock juts out of stone—a hard shape.

3. Growing up

Susquehanna   *Niagara*   *Mohawk*

We were the foreigners who catalogued native streams.
Yet on July afternoons, the reservation was a secret place.

  You were always first in the boat, first out.

  Between two worlds, bailing a leaky boat, rowing,
  we tensed for the shudder of foreign soil.

  Then your hand stretched out from the shore
  and I stretched out my hand, meeting a stranger's.

4. France

High places and rivers: as if an open space might be the truth—
    a flow between dark fields,
    a tall rock in a field of broken stone.

      Climbing toward Madeloc:
          foreground: cork and olive,
          middle distance: grey stone,
          horizon: a toy tower, a panel of washed sky.

    Sometimes we put on truth as if it were a skin
    or touch the truth of things as if they wore a skin of stone.

5. A light within the river tells us who we are.

The trees are plumes of black cloud; the true sky is a patch of broken light.

    But in a mirror bright as polished ice,
    a falling star descends from dark to dark.

    My throat is trembling to the silences within a mirror.
    A light within dark waters is about to speak.

Privacies

1

Doors.
Arriving.   Entering.
Gone.
Again . . .   Gone.
Again.
To be so like, so matched:
    railroad tracks that focus to a V,
        that meet, do not join . . .
    or twins:
        separate, shared . . .
Twins, then.
    One door.   Gone.
Running:
    You on the left, beach road . . . .
    Or at night, narrow place (path by water)
        running on darkness
        footsteps
            (parallels)
    Down.   Down.
        mouths
        doors

2

Here in a drifting landscape of winter and thorn
walls
speak to a man on a hill.
   Below Drumholm
   torn seas crowd
   stone.
      (This limestone pebble ground to my palm . . .
I tell walls names.
           loss

   living room (fireplace) . . .
   front stairs . . .
   head of stairs . . .
    doors
     knob turning
          loss   *loss*

Or within two dreams,
one signpost,
the word obscured, warped letters indecipherable to the rubbing dark.
   . . . or like a stone in my palm
     drilled through by sea worms, a shape
      tumbling in surf,
       a form
         held floating in grey light,
        a grey suspension drifting on storm.

3

In an Irish winter on a windblown hill,
I think of Ogham letters carved on stone,
stone circles, dolmens, standing stones,
a sweaty limestone pebble in a sweaty hand.

It comes so suddenly:
the walls, the room,
the texture of a hand: nothing gone.
As if stone dreamed.

Tonight my mind is full of the ghosts of this hill,
old men and women wrinkled as death,
crisp daughters, sons swollen with dream,
generations of lovers gone under the hill

and the dark that they shared
and their lost names stumbling through night.

Fathers

1

A Ridge of Broken Light

Trees   bent figures hurrying.   Thunder.
We find him in the slant field   earth man.   We bargain for turf.
I am talking to grey eyes and hands.   The hands are sculptured   welts for veins,
panels for skin.   His eyes talk while mouths talk.

The Bargain

Huge stumps come toward my hand   upended roots.
I hear laughter tumbling in thunder.   Laughter.   Old eyes.

This is a dirge.

I write about
a man I do not know,
a man in a field.

Now hands meet.   His fingers are glove leather.

2

Talking about Death

The antiquities of Ireland stain our hands:
dolmens   cairns   headstones.
Our hands are full of death.

        I try to understand feeling

(We lean across a grave slab   bodies taut   brushing off dust.)

        this
        rush of pain
        and love

while we go on talking.

3

My father died.
        She crawled into an attic trunk and pulled down the lid: bang.
                Only a baby.

I yelled and somebody got her out.
        ''Try to be quiet,'' they said.
                So I helped her dress dolls.

        The windows are afraid.   Nobody's home.

I won't ask.
        ''Helen's a baby; you'll be a big boy now.''
                His nice laugh   all muddy.

        The doors and the windows are crying.   I won't ask.

                Someone is walking toward Delaware Avenue,
                street light to street light.
                It is an old coat   out walking.

4

Indian Summer

October haze:
the long fields blackening gold furrows
. . . as if some hazy memory
of last year's frost found speech.

Six feet tall   a big gaunt man   a gaunt lined face   nothing like that father
who is a voice talking in dream   nothing like a man in an Irish field.   I am
reminded by the slant of light on an October hill   by the tilt of a hand in wrecked October.
Thunder.

''It's our last freedom: taking a piss in the woods.''

But in a downpour!   And with a gas station five miles back!

learning to be a man   without baseball or fishing rods

Vermont   New Hampshire   Maine   patches of first snow on the hills   a kind
of autumn leprosy   desperate to piss   afraid to say ''bathroom''

man's talk   talk of cars, women   hard times (bladder ruined)   ''last
gas for 40 miles'' (death by drowning)

and then the rag-tag woods   the deluge   freedom.

Dead now.

A letter: "You have to work at marriage, it's not a present.   There are plenty of good women in this world—enough for any man.   You find one and the two of you work at it.''

A letter: "Tom told me I'd changed his life . . .   a turning point . . .''
Remembering Tom.   Sleepless in a jammed New York hotel.   His alert breathing   the silences between breaths.   My silences my breathing.   "All I'd done was talk to him . . .   He was young; he had everything to live for: an immortal.''

Last letter: "17 nitroglycerine yesterday . . .   Not much longer . . .   a good life . . .   the right woman . . .   a daughter . . .   beautiful . . . fine sons . . .   friends . . .   all the immortals . . .   like sons and daughters to me . . .   unforgettable.''

He called us immortals; he taught us how to use the freedom of a breathing space around our lives.

5

Unpacking Old Albums

without cops and robbers   *without dances*

details of the photograph:

      digging a ditch
          the shovel halfway to my shoulder
              a blur of hair across eyes

      daylilies   phlox   poppies   iris

      the dog's mouth open   a broken leap   ears flying

      nothing fades   light cuts across the island
                            spelling out the names of things
                            a dog's name barking through sky

                      Tell me your darkness,
                      the dark fire troubling a boy's eyes!
                      Who is your mouth calling?

                      I forget me not.

                      These lilies!
                      These gaudy iris:
                          Wabash!
                          Grand Canyon!

names tumbling the hair of my eyes

George   Ellen   Jule   Fran

fixed   flying

I have been set digging by the father of my best friend. He stands outside the photograph, looking on. He knows what I do not know.	*I am a contest. George is judge. The girls are jury. I know about the photograph. The dog is jumping. He spells out his name to the garden.*	*Why am I digging? George's father knows. He has set me digging. He has made me the contest. They are judge and are jury. A father's knowing.*

forget   forget not   forget   forget not   forget   forget not

How can anyone say to the dead, I understand at last?
How can anyone talk to the loneliness of the dead?

     alive and afraid
         my loneliness picks up the empty shovel
         brushes back hair from my eyes
         steps from the photograph

What I cannot say is already said.

It was a way   a kindness   a loneliness used up.

Sometimes I think that life is nothing more than broken melodies in love with song
or an erratic camera that remembers us, if at all, in twisted attitudes
the gratitude unexpressed   not even felt   until darkness drowns a garden's light.

6

Thunder in the leaves of late autumn.   Beyond the ridge   a thundering sea.
I lower myself into the thunder   rung over rung   as over a sea wall   a high wall.
A sea of voices rising from clods and stone speaks to me in the brogue of a Donegal farmer,
gongs and bells and strained planks chorus and choir to a meadow of cattle.

''Talk to me.   Name me, fathers.''   A rubble of sea-borne voices drowned in the
                                                                                                    tide.

I have begun to row   I am drifting out of the bay   rowing against grey music.
Or tides stand still   a streak of late sun under rain clouds
or I have shipped oars   turning sky   my hands pools of last light.
A breeze flickers the wave tops   gauze silence
or a spatter of rain cleans the clay from my hands.

I have become cold as night.

A song of the darkness hangs on the long fields
folds on the fields like slowed waves
turning.

Midwinter

At dusk, a great flare of winter lightning photographed the bay:
Waves were broken scrolls.   Beyond Donegal, white mountains
hung in a narrow bas-relief frozen on sky.

                              Later, there was sleet: trees down
on the Drumholm road; near Timoney's farm, a frantic goose
pinned under branches.

              All night long, we spoke of loneliness,
long winter, while winter sang in the chimneys.

Then the sky cleared and a marvel began: The hills turned blue;
in the valley a blue cottage sent up the day's first plume of smoke.
It gathered like a dream drenched in frost.

That should have been all.   We had worn out night.

But single-file, deliberate, five heifers, a black bull, three calves stepped through the
                                                            broken fence.
They arranged themselves between the house and hedge: a kind of diagram:
a shifting pattern grazing frozen weeds.

Their image is with me still.   The backs of the cattle are patchy with frost blue as
                                                            morning.

Inhabitant

Perhaps there are no more apparitions:

There are no figures at the window,
        none on the stairs,
        none rustling through the narrow spaces inside the walls.

Tonight I shall unlock all of the doors and all of the windows.

Even this chair feels empty.

The Dark Theatre

—for Tom, for Theone

Or driving the Carrick/Killibegs road—
face forward into darkening light,
maneuvering: sheep, cattle:

or, at night, the road twisting Glencar
moonlight, five swans:
a drift of moonlight and feathers,

      long necks dipping silence:

or predawn grey cats
hurtling abrupt intricate diagrams
through Sligo streets—

      as if there were a theatre out there,
      our silences listening to the charged darkness.

      The comedians'
      long necks arched above water, cats' paws, retractable nails
      cannot transform blank eyes.

      I study actors' eyes,
      knowing your eyes follow them,
      questioning.

          . . . I'll tell you no lies.

The touch of failed light on a black ridge,
the fallen moon a fanlight over Glencar,
touches us who do not touch here in this rented car.

.   .   .   .

Theone, Tom, love is enough/not enough.

If there were waterfalls (starbursts) of descending light . . .

I say over your names, over and over,
yet dawn spells out the shape of my hand in this dark place,
and I know who we are (separate   each   ), who I am.

Separate

1. Pennsylvania

Fragments of love.   Like petals after the storm.
They lie on silvery grass
full of magic, resonant.   Stars:
the shape of constellations: arbitrary as that.

I remember lying there drenched in sweat,
coupled to you, full of love,
our bodies busy as oiled gears.

Yet animals filed in—zebra, giraffe, lion—
wallpaper octagons putting on form.

Our minds do that: the mosaic full of demands,
a child on a sweaty bed,
a fever thermometer in his mouth.   Blue lions, roaring.

2. Grafton

All day long the hill has been wrapped in rain.
But now there is a diagram:
two trees carved from green ice
touch.

I take your hand in my hand.
It is fragile,
trembling in the stillness of lost light.

We are filled with the ache and loneliness of love.

3. Ireland

If I imagine you, it is as a figure on the great arc of sand beyond Ballintra.
You are out of hearing.   Or at Rossnowlagh, out of hearing and sight.

You walk along the tide rim of the world.

4.

A zodiac of petals: blue zebra.   The wall.

Han Dynasty

They are jugs. They are owls.
Their mouths are mouths.

They overflow silence;
we see them through glass.

Your eyes are owl eyes
drinking silence.

I rub my hands on the dark
as if on smeared glass.

Stone Beach: Connemara

Tide's out: stone clinging to rusty sunlight

(soft folds under stone or hidden under stones of ribbed tidepools
or hidden on the undersides of kelp),

salt tides, salt drying: red kelp gone black.

''We know each other too well,'' you say.
All right.   Amen to that!

It is as if the rinsed dry shelves of a stony place voice our demands
or as if the angry gulls put on our narrowest hungers in their calling.

''Nevertheless . . .''

On the stone beach at Collioure we oiled stone pebbles, polishing them on slippery skin.
Or on the Straits of Juan de Fuca walked on sea-rubbed stones so effortlessly glazed they
                                        might press oil . . . .

Under dry kelp, dark silence darkens stone.
Under sunburned stones, mouths rub wet furrows
waiting tide's turn and the floodtide sea.

Sleepless

1.   10:00 P.M.   lake shore/ridge/seashore

Shadows drift out of quarter light.
''Evening . . .''   shadowy voices   ''Evening''   stroking our voices.
We walk along night's border, listening to a hazy evening drift across a lake.
Frog splash.   Cattle silhouetted on a ridge trail toward the sea.
We have become private in diminished light:
interior   separate   as inarticulate as standing stone.

2.   3:15 A.M.   The Window

Long swells of the sea unfold.   Long clouds invent a definition of the sea.

Perhaps moon, tracing out a pattern on thin clouds, has set you walking on this pebbled
                                                                              beach.

      I hear you toss in sleep behind me.

Out there in moonlight, there is a sudden hollow in the stones.
It is as if sea caves have given way, collapsing yards of beach.
I am afraid.   You climb down toward a pool of salty moonlight,
moon vanishing behind a cloud.
                              Now you are a part of darkness.
I stretch my hand down the salt emptiness, but the tips of fingers vanish.
They have entered ink.   Invisible, helpless, they stir blind silence.

      Behind me, you moan in sleep, lost.   . . . drowning?

3.   Vulnerable

Two children asleep on a wide bed:
the boy eleven or twelve, barely adolescent,
his sister, a year or two younger, curled asleep,
already girl-woman.

I am father/mother/brother/sister.

They fall in toward themselves, the girl's soft hair brushing his shoulder.

If I should die before I wake . . .

. . . boy hand pressed to the small of her back,
her mouth asking questions of salt skin,
the chords of a long throat
. . . taste and texture.

Love me or I die

. . . not love exactly, not death
. . . turning
returning . . .

4.

Lake water:

androgynous lover
bent above water
his boy's mouth
pressed to her mouth.

5.   Vulnerable

The liars: father and mother
folding into themselves
conception's terror/duty:

alive.

Taste this.

First:

held off   waiting   a wait,

sea caves falling.

.   .   .   .   .   .

Or to fold into yourself . . .
     not fetus, not child,
  a soft uncovering dream—
        as a hand fallen open to dawn:
        dark hair spread on the whitening pillow, dark eyes still dreaming

            waves folded under—
              loops and whorls . . .

then dandelion sky: loose puffs of air—   light's carnival.

"I love you" too easy in an abandon of beginnings, incense, and origins.

But fragile as a prayer of unfoldings:

       cry of gull, child's cry . . .

           tender as the light of morning on long grass,
           two children sleeping in one vulnerable smile,
           articulate, lonely, lovely, perishable:

                              this choice.

Souterrain

1

Tunnel or grave?
We kneel in a landscape of dung and wet heather,
hair streaming rain,
to push back grass.

The lintel is glazed in mud.
Our hands skid on stone.
We push back grass. Then it is clear,
shining: a body in the fields.

Certainly it is like a body stretched out in quiet rain
hungering earth.
We touch hands to stone
as if a dying heart churned its whiteness.

2

A rush of blood in the ears,
a pulse of darkness.

Down.

An artery pulsing darkness.

What does the heart know in a hole in the ground?

I listen for truth—
a pebble displaced.

    The dead make love:
    clavicle   femur   metatarsus   ribs
    three wrecked hands
                    tangled.

    Must we give them names?

Lights out. I listen for heartbeat,
hearts beating.
                    In a jumble of dead bones,
the heart's darkness.

3

To be an other in a strange place,
that is dread.
        Tonight I am at peace.
        I move from room to room
        of a firelit house on a hill
        loving the silences
        friends share who have worn out speech:

                        geometries of light.

Or a lost one in search of himself
confused by blind hands:
grave furniture: toys.

  The blunder of walls
        all fours

  baby?

        (mama . . .   papa . . .   mama . . .

  Bones.

  Other.   Other.

A self, then.

. . . planes of affection and light
flickering
silence.

Wet stone

mama . . .   mama . . .

The dark.

4

All the goodbyes of the world
come to a Donegal hillside in August rain.
''You do a job, you want to do it good'':
four extra sacks of clay on a rain-soaked grave.

In a neighboring pasture, the lintel,
an earth-clogged door, a hole:
''A good place to play. But candles go out.
We never went far.'' Her brother: ''He's dead now, a good man.''
''A good son to me,'' a ragged voice from the dark beyond firelight.

Fragments:
    Socrates gnawing *the good*, an old dog worrying a new bone;
    '' 'Tis new to thee'';
    a night swim out from Oran.

Mouth against mouth, skin on skin, *the good life*, we say; *I love you*, we say, to the dark-
                                             ness filling our arms.

On a Donegal hillside a little crowd of broken skulls peers from the rubble of a broken
                                                   tomb.

5

September.   Then the long winter dreaming of spring.

Turning.   Brightening.   Like folds of winter earth turning before the plow,

or like a restless sleeper who exhausts dream's ritual.

Clouds turn beneath dawn wind.

An edge of light restores the shape of stone.

Notes

The Burn. The poem is assumed to take place during a westbound flight from Ireland to Canada. Sligo, where Yeats spent his childhood, is on the west coast of Ireland. Mountrath is about halfway between Dublin and Limerick. Jonathan Swift is, of course, buried in St. Patrick's Cathedral, Dublin. First published, *Poetry Northwest*, 17, no. 2 (Summer 1976).

Gunsight. In press, *Poetry Now*.

At Renvyle. Renvyle is the westernmost tip of Connemara and the site of Oliver St. John Gogarty's estate, now an exceptionally pleasant hotel. First published, *The Arts in Ireland*, 1, no. 2 (Winter 1972-1973):34.

Below the Cliffs, Donegal. First published, *The Arts in Ireland*, 1, no. 2 (Winter 1972-1973):34.

Tír Conaill. Tír Conaill is the original Irish name for the area now called Donegal. Scattered all over the county are great megalithic dolmens, huge stone burial chambers. A number of them are called ''Grania's bed,'' in commemoration of the legend that the fleeing lovers—pursued by Grania's husband—were forced each night to make a bed in a new location. First published, *The Arts in Ireland*, 1, no. 2 (Winter 1972-1973):35.

Before Dawn. First published, *Wind*, no. 19 (1975):50.

Beach. Annick Chapoy is a French journalist whom I had met casually at the Yeats International Summer School. A group of her friends celebrated her birthday by presenting her with homemade gifts. I offered a poem but said she'd have to wait for it to be written. *Beach* was to be the poem but turned into something far different. Another attempt at it became *Bridge: Sligo*. It finally was written—just a year late—as *August 22*. Roger Conover, the American poet, was spending a year in Ireland when I met him in the summer of 1972. His wife's name is Anna. My former wife's name is Ann. First published, *The Arts in Ireland*, 1, no. 3 (1973):66.

August 22. First published, *Poetry Northwest*, 15, no. 2 (Summer 1974):28.

Song at Drumholm. Drumholm is a very sparsely populated area southwest of the city of Donegal. Rog Conover, for whom this song was written, spent most of a winter there. I was a frequent visitor. First published, *Shenandoah: The Washington and Lee Review*, 25, no. 4 (Summer 1974):45.

Apology at Midnight. Hokusai (1760-1849) is, of course, the great Japanese printmaker. In press, *Poetry Now*.

Natural History. The Natural History section of Ireland's National Museum can be entered only from Merrion Street. The main entrance to the Museum is on Kildare Street. The Museum of Science that I mention in the second stanza is in Buffalo, New York. First published, *Poetry Ireland*, no. 5 (Spring 1965):1-2.

Irish Winter. Coole Park was the home of Augusta Gregory, Yeats's close friend and frequent collaborator. Though the house itself is gone, the red gate to the walled garden still survives—as does its echo. Newgrange, the great megalithic tomb above the Boyne Valley, was several years ago discovered to have a precise astronomical orientation. Sheila-na-gig is sometimes represented in Medieval Irish sculpture as a fierce female figure with exaggerated mouth and genitals; she is assumed to warn of the horrors that go with sins of the flesh. First published, *Quarterly Review of Literature*, 14, nos. 1-2 (1966):202-203.

North of Collioure, North of Dublin, North of Malahide. During the autumn and early winter of 1964, my wife and I lived in the coastal town of Malahide about ten miles north of Dublin. Just north of Malahide was a small spit of land that projected out into the Irish Sea. In approximately 2,000 B.C. it had been inhabited by a pre-Celtic race about whom almost nothing is known. For us, this ''peninsula fort'' was an ideal picnic spot. In January we left Malahide for Collioure, a fishing village in the Catalan area of France. First published, *Shenandoah: The Washington and Lee Review*, 16, no. 4 (Summer 1965):96-97.

Morning. First published, *Shenandoah: The Washington and Lee Review*, 24, no. 4 (Summer 1974):60.

A Poem for Liam Miller. Liam Miller is the book designer, publisher, and architect who founded Dolmen Press. Phil Ryan's pub was located on Lower Baggot Street, not far from Liam's old address. I had first sailed to Ireland on the *America,* where I met the Irish girl returning to Kerry. The poem is a montage of places: Dublin/New York in my memory, Paris/Dublin in Liam's. First published, *Southern Poetry Review*, 11, no. 1 (Fall 1970):6-8.

Dublin Evening, Afternoon near Clifden. Clifden is the largest city in western Connemara. Jane, mentioned in the poem, is Liam Miller's daughter. First published, *Wind*, 5, no. 19 (1975):49-50.

Bridge: Sligo. First published, *CAIM*, 3, no. 1 (1976).

Rivers, High Places. Lough Allen is about twenty miles west and a bit north of Sligo. Madeloc is a tower on a peak of the Pyrenees. It overlooks the Mediterranean fishing village of Collioure. First published, *Greenfield Review*, 5, nos. 1-2 (Summer 1976).

Privacies. The unclosed parenthesis is a matter of author's choice rather than proofreader's chance. First published *Bird Effort*, nos. 3-4 (1976).

Fathers. I've always distrusted elegies. I think one should write poems for the living rather than the dead. And yet when I heard that Pearley Perkins had died, I started this one. Pearley had been debate coach at Middlebury College when I was an undergraduate there. During the four years that I attended Middlebury, he became a kind of surrogate father. My own father had died when I was four, and I think now that I must have spent a good deal of my time searching for a replacement. The first one I'd found was Edwin Weinheimer, the father of my closest high school friend, George, and of the three girls— Ellen, Jule, and Fran—who are mentioned in part 5 of the poem. While I was working on the poem, Edwin Weinheimer also died. The two deaths, so close together, forced me back to the fragmented memory of my own father's death, a death I'd been unable to cope with when I was a child and that is still marked in my memory only by a sense of absence. All that I can remember of the day of his death is a moment when my two-year-old sister was trapped in an attic trunk. The enclosing sections of the poem (1, 2, and 6) are set in Ireland. The figure in the first part is a farmer from whom we bought peat and who raised spectacularly good carrots. He seemed in a number of ways an Irish equivalent of Maine-born Pearley Perkins. Tom, mentioned in section 4, was a troubled boy who had been befriended by Pearley and who valued him, I know, as much as I did. The poem tries to say what I was never able to say directly to Pearley Perkins or Edwin Weinheimer. Previously unpublished.

Midwinter. Timoney's farm is in Drumholm. The family supplied us with milk and much good companionship. First published, *Interstate*, 2, no. 1 (1976):89.

Inhabitant. First published, *The Arts in Ireland*, 2, no. 4 (1974):68. Revised version, published, *Wind*, 5, no. 19 (1975):51.

The Dark Theatre. The Carrick/Killibegs road is in Donegal. Glencar is a waterfall, pool, and lake not far from Sligo. Yeats, who frequently visited the spot, celebrated it in his early poetry. Theone Trapatsos Bob and Tom Tavis are friends who in 1975 joined me for part of a summer in Ireland. First published, *The Anglo-Welsh Review*, 26, no. 57 (Summer 1976).

Separate. Rossnowlagh is on the Donegal coast several miles south of the village of Ballintra. First published, *Modern Poetry Studies*, 7, no. 2 (Summer 1976). Section 3 was first published in the *Ark River Review*, 3, no. 1 (1974):23, under the title *Ireland*.

Han Dynasty. First published, *Wind*, 5, no. 19 (1975):50.

Stone Beach: Connemara. One stone beach leads to another. Collioure's is in southern France and the one on the Straits of Juan de Fuca in the state of Washington. First published, *Hawaii Review*, no.7, (Autumn 1976).

Sleepless. First published, *Choice*, no. 10 (1976).

Souterrain. Ireland is pockmarked with holes—most of them man-made and many of them burial places. The great cairns of the west and east coasts—artificial hills with low tunnels into cruciform chambers—and such souterrains as those constructed during Viking times for the secret disposition of abbey treasures seem to open up doorways: into the past, into the earth, into death. Many such underground passages are neglected, still full of their own privacies. The fragments in part 4 are, of course, drawn from the Socratic dialogues, *The Tempest*, and Camus' *The Plague*. First published, *The Anglo-Welsh Review*, 24, no. 53 (Winter 1974):139-41.

✕ Production Notes

This book was typeset on the Unified Composing System *(Compugraphic)* at The University Press of Hawaii.

The design is by Larry Cooke and the text typeface is Holland Seminar. Display matter is set in Korinna.

Offset printing and binding is the work of Thomson-Shore, Inc.

Text paper is Perkins & Squier Old Forge Book Laid, basis 65.